OHIO

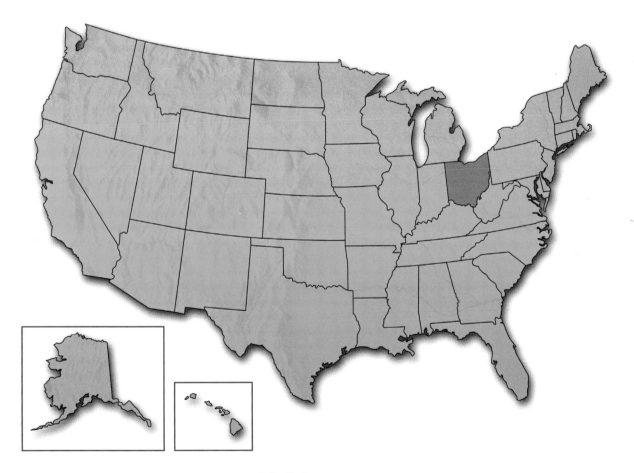

Val Lawton

Published by Weigl Publishers Inc.
123 South Broad Street, Box 227
Mankato, MN   56002
USA
Web site: http://www.weigl.com

Library of Congress Cataloging-in-Publication Data

Lawton, Val.
    Ohio / Val Lawton.
       p. cm. -- (A kid's guide to American states)
    Includes bibliographical reference and index.
    ISBN 1-930954-03-4
       1. Ohio--Juvenile literature. [1. Ohio.] I. title. II. Series.

F491.3 .L39 2001

2001026000

ISBN 1-930954-93-X

Printed in the United States of America
1 2 3 4 5 6 7 8 9 10   05 04 03 02 01

Project Coordinator
Jennifer Nault
Substantive Editor
Leslie Strudwick
Copy Editor
Heather Kissock
Designers
Warren Clark
Terry Paulhus
Photo Researcher
Angela Lowen

Photograph Credits
Every reasonable effort has been made to trace ownership and to obtain permission to reprint copyright material. The publishers would be pleased to have any errors or omissions brought to their attention so that they may be corrected in subsequent printings.

Cover: Girl Picking Apples (Mark E. Gibson/The Image Finders), Buckeye Tree (Jim Baron/The Image Finders); **Archive Photos:** pages 15BL, 21BL, 25T; **1-800-BUCKEYE www.OhioTourism.com:** pages 3T, 4T, 4BR, 5BL, 7T, 8T, 8BL, 8BR, 10T, 12T, 16T, 16BL, 20T, 20B, 21T, 26B, 27B; **Jim Baron/The Image Finders:** pages 3M, 4BL, 5T, 10BR, 14BR, 22T, 22B, 25BL; **Rita Byron/The Image Finders:** page 23BR; **Carillon Historical Park:** page 6BR; **Corbis Corporation:** page 13T; **Corel Corporation:** pages 10BL, 14BL, 26T; **Dublin Irish Festival:** page 23BL; **Michael Evans/The Image Finders:** pages 9T, 15BR; **EyeWire Corporation:** pages 28TL, 29B; **Mark E. Gibson/The Image Finders:** page 15T; **Jeff Greenberg/The Image Finders:** pages 16BR, 23T, 29T; **David Haas/The Image Finders:** page 12BL; **Greg Hildebrandt/The Image Finders:** pages 9BL, 25BR; **J. Leary/Bruce Bennett Studios:** page 27ML; **Angela Lowen:** page 6BL; **Marion Popcorn Festival:** page 24T; **Ohio State Governors Office:** page 7B; **Ohio State Historical Society:** pages 17T, 17B, 18T, 18B, 19T, 19BL, 19BR; **PhotoDisc Corporation:** page 14T; **Photofest:** pages 24BL, 28B; **Charles Robinson:** pages 3B, 24BR; **Stata Productions/The Image Finders:** page 9BR; **Carl A. Stimac/The Image Finders:** page 21BR; **Wagner Photography/The Image Finders:** page 13B; **Mark and Sue Werner/The Image Finders:** pages 6T, 11T, 11B; **Frank Wiewandt/The Image Finders:** page 12BR.

CONTENTS

INTRODUCTION

An mile-long boardwalk guides visitors through the Cedar Bog Nature Preserve, which has many rare plants and animals.

Ohio is a remarkable state, with rich farmland, beautiful scenery, exciting cities, and a well-preserved history. It is known as a Great Lake state, because it is partly bordered by Lake Erie. Ohio's geographic location makes the state an important crossroads in the nation's east. Early settlers developed transportation routes between Lake Erie to the north and the Ohio River to the south.

Ohio is known for its flat prairie land, but the state is also famous for a tall, triangular structure that is found in Cleveland. The Rock and Roll Hall of Fame and Museum houses exhibits that showcase rock and roll's greats, such as Elvis Presley and Tina Turner. Unlike most states, Ohio even has an official rock song, called "Hang on Sloopy." Many people visit the Rock and Roll Hall of Fame to learn about the legendary musicians that have made rock and roll one of the most popular forms of music in the world.

QUICK FACTS

Ohio became the seventeenth state to join the Union on March 1, 1803.

The state motto, "With God, All Things are Possible," was not adopted until 1958, well after most other states had chosen their mottos.

People who live in Ohio are called "Ohioans" and "Buckeyes."

The name *Ohio* comes from an Iroquois-Seneca word that means "beautiful river."

Cincinnati is the third-largest city in Ohio. The city has been a major port on the Ohio River for many years.

The Cleveland Hopkins International Airport has more than 600 airplanes arriving and departing every day.

QUICK FACTS

The state stone is flint, a type of quartz found in many colors. Native Americans made spear points and arrowheads out of this stone.

Ohio's state song, "Beautiful Ohio," was written in honor of the Ohio River, not for the state.

Ohio's official nickname is "The Buckeye State" in honor of the buckeye tree, which grows throughout the area.

Ohio has two state flowers: the red carnation, in honor of President William McKinley, and the trillium grandiflorum.

Getting There

The state of Ohio shares its borders with Michigan and Lake Erie to the north, and Kentucky and West Virginia to the south. Indiana is to the west, and Pennsylvania is to the east.

There are many ways to reach Ohio. Travelers arriving by air can land in many different Ohio cities, including Akron, Dayton, Toledo, and Columbus. The busiest airports are in Cleveland and Columbus. The Cleveland Hopkins International Airport serves the greater Cleveland area.

For those who prefer to travel by automobile, there are interstate highways going in all directions. Travelers can also reach most Ohio cities and towns by bus. For train travelers, Amtrak has two routes that cross through Ohio. There is also a ferry that runs between Augusta, Kentucky and Higginsport, Ohio.

Ohio Location Map

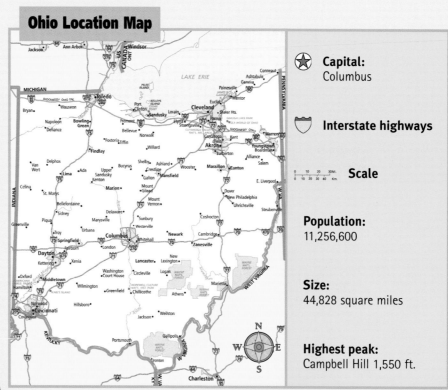

⭐ **Capital:**
Columbus

🛡 **Interstate highways**

Scale

Population:
11,256,600

Size:
44,828 square miles

Highest peak:
Campbell Hill 1,550 ft.

Ohio's state bird is the cardinal. It was adopted in 1933. The cardinal is known for its clear, strong song and brilliant plumage.

Some residents of Ohio have made important inventions and significant discoveries. Before Henry Ford introduced his first automobile, John Lambert chugged down the streets of Ohio City in the nation's first gas-powered car in 1891. Only a few years earlier, in 1876, the state witnessed the birth of electricity with the first commercial arc lamp. This lamp was exhibited in Cleveland by Charles F. Brush. The state also saw the nation's first traffic light in 1914.

You may think of Ohio the next time you board an airplane. One of the greatest inventions of the twentieth century originated in Ohio. Dayton's Orville and Wilbur Wright, better known as the "Wright Brothers," flew the world's first airplane. Although it took several attempts, on December 17, 1903, Orville managed to get the airplane into the sky—for a thrilling 12 seconds! The United States has the Wright Brothers to thank for its strong name in **aviation**.

QUICK FACTS

Columbus is Ohio's state capital.

Neil Armstrong, the first man to walk on the moon, was from Wapakoneta, Ohio.

Always fascinated by mechanics, the Wright Brothers repaired bicycles in their own bicycle shop before they became interested in flying.

Peppermint Lifesavers were introduced by a Cleveland chocolate manufacturer in 1913.

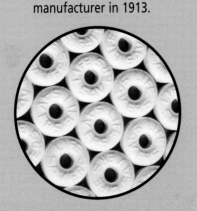

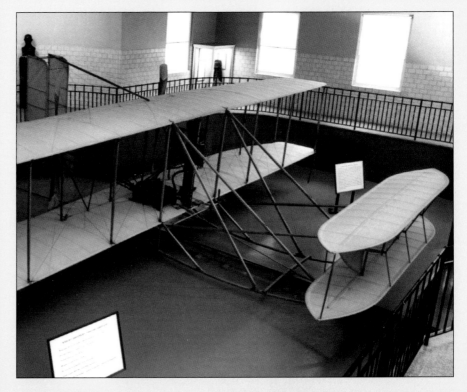

The 1905 Wright Flyer III is housed in Wright Hall at Carillon Historical Park in Dayton, Ohio. It was the world's first plane capable of controlled flight.

Ohio has one of the most unique state flags in the nation. Its flag is the only one in the United States that is not rectangular in shape. Instead, Ohio's flag is pennant-shaped. The flag was adopted by an Act of the Ohio Legislature on May 9, 1902. It has three red and two white horizontal stripes and a blue triangle. The triangle represents hills and valleys, and the stripes stand for roads and waterways. There are also seventeen white stars gathered around an "O." Thirteen of the stars stand for the original states of the Union. Surrounding the thirteen stars are four more stars. When added, these stars represent Ohio's status as the seventeenth state admitted into the Union.

Ohio's state seal is also unique. It has gone through many changes over the years, but the final version became official in 1967. It has a sheaf of wheat, representing Ohio's strength in agriculture. A bundle of seventeen arrows stand for Ohio's rank in the Union. Thirteen rays around the sun represent the original colonies of the United States.

QUICK FACTS

There are 44,000 miles of rivers and streams in Ohio.

Lake Erie and the Ohio River are natural features that serve as state boundaries.

The Ohio River is a source of drinking water for more than 3 million people.

The Ohio coat of arms is quite similar to Ohio's seal. The only difference between the two is that the phrase "The Great Seal of the State of Ohio" is not present on the coat of arms.

Winter temperatures in Ohio range from 24°F to 35°F.

LAND AND CLIMATE

Ohio is comprised of three major land regions. They are the Lake Plains, the Central Plains, and the Allegheny Plateau. The highest point of land in Ohio is Campbell Hill at 1,550 feet.

Slow-moving glaciers that covered much of North America are responsible for Ohio's rich soil. Glaciers that blanketed about two-thirds of the state shaped the land into gently rolling hills. The melting glaciers created swamps and bogs. Later, when the areas drained, fertile soil remained.

Ohio has cold winters and warm summers. There is a large amount of snow in the winter, and the month of June has the greatest rainfall. For many years, Ohio has struggled with spring flooding. Since the mid-1900s, Ohioans have widened riverbanks and constructed dams and reservoirs to help manage spring floods.

Glacial grooves provide evidence of the last glacial ice sheet that left Ohio 15,000 years ago.

NATURAL RESOURCES

Ohio contributes about 3 percent of the total coal produced in the United States.

Ohioans recognized the importance of their mineral resources during the 1800s. At this time, residents discovered that nearly half of the state sat on large pockets of petroleum oil, natural gas, and coal. By the late 1800s, there were many active coal mines in the state. Coal, petroleum oil, and natural gas are still found in Ohio.

Many minerals are taken from the earth for industrial use. Ohio's most important mineral is limestone—the Buckeye State ranks second in the nation in limestone production. Limestone is a **sedimentary** rock that is useful in building materials. Some varieties of limestone are used in flooring and monuments. Other industrial minerals from Ohio include shale, salt, clay, sand, gravel, sandstone, gypsum, and peat.

QUICK FACTS

Ohio ranks third nationally in the production of construction sand and gravel.

There is no large production of precious gems in Ohio.

Most of the state's limestone comes from northwestern and central Ohio.

Ohio has a long shoreline bordering Lake Erie. For many years, the water quality had been quite poor due to industrial and urban waste. Fish populations had been steadily declining in these waters until efforts were made to clean the lake. By the early 1990s, recreational fishing had resumed along Ohio's shoreline.

Walleye, smallmouth bass, and perch are just some of the types of fish that sport fishers can find in Lake Erie.

PLANTS AND ANIMALS

Hemlock and birch trees can be found in Conkles Hollow.

From dense forests to open prairies, Ohio offers an array of plant life, which supports a large variety of animal life. Forests in Ohio are found primarily in the state's southern and eastern areas. In many other parts of the state, farming has replaced most of the original forest lands. Hardwood trees common to the state include oaks, maples, hickories, black maples, and sycamores. Virginia pines and white pines are just some of the **conifers** that grow in the area.

The buckeye tree is found mostly near rivers and in moist areas. It can grow up to 70 feet tall, and bears yellow flowers. Although these flowers are quite beautiful, they have an unpleasant odor.

Springtime brings an array of forest wildflowers to Ohio. It is not unusual to spot violets, mayapples, hepaticas, and bloodroot in the spring. In the fall, many wildflowers, such as black-eyed Susans and goldenrods, grow in open spaces.

Ohio has a mild autumn because it is bordered by Lake Erie. Large bodies of water help keep the climate temperate.

Ohio's white-tailed deer have home ranges of only 2 to 3 square miles, which they occupy year-round.

Originally, Ohio was home to many large mammals, including the bison, elk, black bear, timber wolf, and cougar. Today, the white-tailed deer is the only large mammal found in the state. In fact, there are more white-tailed deer than any other wild animal in Ohio. Rabbits, wild turkeys, pheasants, and partridges are just some of the small animals in the state. Other small mammals include moles, muskrats, beavers, and opossums.

Since Ohio lies beneath the Mississippi Flyway, a major bird migration route, bird-watchers may catch a glimpse of as many as 350 different kinds of birds soaring overhead. They should also be on the lookout for about 180 different bird species that are native to Ohio.

There are many varieties of fish in the state's rivers. They include bass, northern pike, walleye, and muskellunge. In the north, Lake Erie is home to walleye, lake trout, and some salmon species. Each year, Ohio sport fishers catch more than 25 million fish in Lake Erie.

Raccoon

TOURISM

The state is brimming with fascinating sites for for visitors to examine. Ohio has three national historic sites. At Hopewell Cultural National Park, tourists can learn about the ancient mound-building Hopewell culture that inhabited the region until about 500 AD. They can even view a 2,000-year-old mound. The other two historic sites in Ohio mark and preserve places of great national interest: the birthplace of President William H. Taft and the home of President James A. Garfield.

Ohio has one international monument—Perry's Victory and International Peace Monument. It is located on South Bass Island, which is part of the Lake Erie Isles. This monument stands 352 feet tall. This granite tower offers a spectacular view of the western tip of Lake Erie. It was named after the United States naval officer, Oliver H. Perry. Perry led his sailors to victory in the War of 1812.

Of the remaining 840 covered wooden bridges in the United States, 136 of them are found in Ohio.

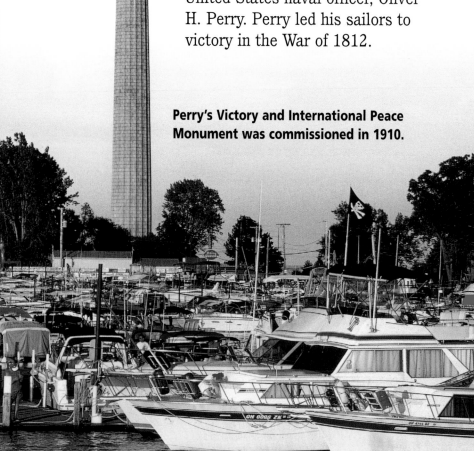

Perry's Victory and International Peace Monument was commissioned in 1910.

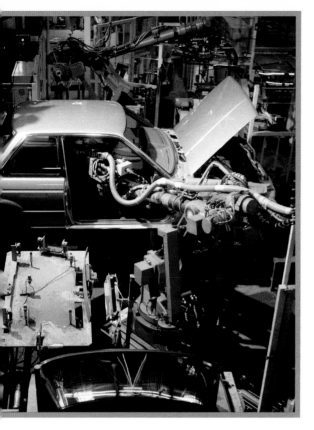

Ohio is one of the top states in automobile manufacturing. Large companies such as Ford and Honda have plants there.

INDUSTRY

From tires, to tractors, to automobiles, many of Ohio's industries keep the nation on the move. Before the onset of **industrialization**, farm equipment manufacturing was one of Ohio's main industries. Still, by the 1890s, Ohioans had developed other important industries besides those linked to agriculture.

Today, Ohio ranks third in the nation for income earned from industrial activity. The state is a major contributor of rubber and plastic products within the nation. Ohio has a long history in rubber manufacturing, with some impressive developments in tire production. Charles Goodyear of Akron came up with the process of **vulcanizing** rubber in 1839. In 1900, the Firestone Tire and Rubber Company, also from Ohio, developed a way to attach tires to removable rims.

The automotive industry in the United States employs many Ohioans. Workers shape and stamp metal parts to make automobile **components**. Metalworkers also manufacture sheet metal and hand tools.

QUICK FACTS

Ohio manufactures transportation equipment, including motor vehicles, motorcycles, and aircraft engines.

In the 1830s, Cincinnati was nicknamed "Porkopolis" for the large number of slaughterhouses in the city.

John Chapman, better known as Johnny Appleseed, brought Ohio farmers apple seeds, founding Ohio's first apple orchards. Some think that his ghost can be seen wandering through Ohio's apple country.

The first concrete road in the United States was an 8-foot stretch of road in Bellefontaine. It was paved by the Buckeye Cement Company in 1891.

Goodyear, a company that originated in Ohio, built its first blimp in 1925. They have since built more than 300 blimps.

The Ohio State Barber Board was established in 1934 to monitor and license members of the barber industry.

GOODS AND SERVICES

Ohio's workforce numbers about 5.8 million people. Government employs 12 percent of the state's workers. Manufacturing employs about 17 percent of Ohio's workforce, while farming provides jobs for only 2 percent. This is a large shift from Ohio's early days, when farming was the population's main occupation. The largest segment, about 29 percent, is employed in the service sector. Nurses, schoolteachers, barbers, and dry cleaners are all members of this sector.

Providing jobs for 23 percent of the state's workforce, wholesale and retail trade trails closely behind the service industry. Agricultural and manufactured products are shipped to all parts of the United States. Cleveland, Columbus, and Cincinnati are the major trade centers, with main exports including machinery, transportation equipment, fabricated metals, and rubber products.

QUICK FACTS

The state beverage is tomato juice, because Ohio produces the most tomato juice in the country.

In 1992, Ohio produced more than 100 million pounds of popping corn on nearly 29,000 acres of land.

About 19 percent of Ohio's workers are **unionized.**

Steel is produced in Ohio for use in computers, booster rockets, and automobiles.

There are about 381 newspapers published in Ohio, and 78 of them are dailies.

Half of the state's farm income is obtained from soybeans, corn, and greenhouse and nursery products. Ohio is a major producer of greenhouse and nursery products in the United States. Many farms in the state are devoted to **floriculture**. These farms provide plant bedding, potted flowering plants, and cut flowers.

Ohioans have access to a variety of communication services, as they have many newspapers and television and radio stations. The state has earned a good reputation in the newspaper industry. At least two significant newspaper chains began in Ohio. As well, the state has been home to some highly acclaimed editors and journalists.

QUICK FACTS

Over 1,700 people worked for many years to build Great Lake St. Mary's, which was completed in 1845. At the time, it was the world's largest human-made lake.

Specialty crops produced in the state include sorghum, canola, and wheat varieties such as emmer and spelt. Other important crops include tomatoes and grapes.

A native of Ohio, Whitelaw Reid was a highly respected journalist who wrote for the Washington Tribune.

Ohio State University offers programs in floriculture because the state has such a strong presence in this industry.

In Dublin, Ohio, there is a 12-foot-high sculpture of Wyandot Chief Leatherlips.

QUICK FACTS

Scientists have found Native-American carvings of human and animal figures on a large rock. The site, in Erie County, is now known as Inscription Rock.

The Miami established villages in western Ohio in the valleys of three rivers. These three rivers were called Great Miami, Little Miami, and Miami of the Lake.

The Miamisburg Mound is the largest conical burial mound in the state of Ohio.

FIRST NATIONS

People have lived in present-day Ohio for more than 12,000 years. The first to settle in the region were the Adena. They left behind pottery, evidence of crops, and large mounds that can still be seen today. The Adena were Ohio's first farmers.

The Hopewell lived in parts of southern and central Ohio. Like the Adena, they were a mound-building culture, and built large and impressive structures for worship and social gatherings. They made ornaments from flint, mica, copper, shells, and animal teeth and claws. They lived in the area from 100 BC to 500 AD.

By the late 1690s, Native Americans from other areas began entering Ohio, attracted by its forests and grasslands. The Mingo, related to the Iroquois, lived in the upper Ohio Valley. The Shawnee entered from the south, the Miami arrived from the west, and the Ottawa and the Wyandot entered from the north. Before long, these groups were uprooted and overpowered by the well-organized Six Nations, also known as the Iroquois Confederacy. The Iroquois Confederacy had the first democracy. This meant that all members of the group were given a voice in important decisions.

The Mound Builders left ornaments, jewelry, tools, and ceramic figurines in their mounds.

The Battle of Fallen Timbers was fought between the European settlers and Native Americans who were British allies.

EXPLORERS AND MISSIONARIES

The first known European to arrive in Ohio was French explorer René-Robert Cavelier, also known as Sieur de La Salle. He arrived in the mid-1600s. Next, Joseph de Beinville came to the Dayton area and claimed it for France. The French established fur trading with the Native Peoples and built many wooden trading forts along Ohio's river routes.

More fur traders began to enter the region in 1685. The French and the Native Peoples tried to drive them out, but were unsuccessful. After the American Revolution, the territory became a part of the United States. Ohio's first permanent settlement was at Marietta in 1788. Although the settlement was first called Muskingum, it was renamed Marietta on July 2, 1788.

Many of the missionaries who moved to Ohio came from Saxony, Germany. Missionaries who settled in Ohio in the eighteenth century were known as Moravians. They brought Christianity to many of the Native Americans, such as the Delaware.

Fort Washington

QUICK FACTS

Marietta was Ohio's first permanent settlement. Founded in 1788, it was named in honor of Marie Antoinette, the Queen of France at that time.

The first French fur traders to Ohio built forts along the rivers, but they did not venture inland.

Cincinnati was founded near Fort Washington. Settlers often situated themselves near military forts for safety.

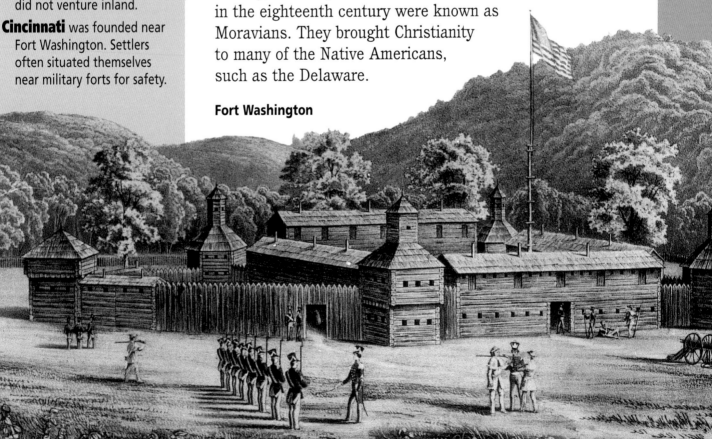

Before moving on to other parts of the United States, many early German settlers first lived in Ohio.

EARLY SETTLERS

Ohio's early settlements were located in a region known as Appalachia. Settlers came from Germany, Ireland, France, Scotland, England, and Sweden. Many Amish settlers came from Switzerland. Most of the American settlers came from New England, in northeastern United States.

A group known as Utopians believed that Ohio was the best place to establish their own **Utopia**. One of their main ambitions was to live in tightly knit communities in the countryside, without interference from outsiders. They believed in sharing responsibility and property equally among the community.

Another well-known Utopian group were the Shakers, a Christian **sect** that came to the United States in the late 1700s. They believed in the sharing of property and in living simply, without showiness.

Amish settlers first came to Ohio in 1803, the same year that Ohio became a state.

In the 1850s, most families in Ohio were full-time farmers.

The British government passed a law to keep settlers from moving west of the Appalachian Mountains. Still, many colonists did not pay attention to this law.

The first oil well in the country was drilled near Caldwell in 1812.

George Armstrong Custer, a Union general, was born in New Rumley, Ohio in 1839. He was defeated at the Battle of the Little Bighorn in 1876.

Though it was the French who first explored the Ohio region, it was the British who settled the area. But it was not long before the area became populated by people from different parts of Europe. Ohio's fertile farmlands began to attract people who were living in other parts of the United States. New Englanders settled in southeast Ohio, and eastern Ohio attracted Quakers from the south and mid-Atlantic region. Virginian settlers arrived in southern Ohio in the late 1700s. Other people living in the south, including people of African-American and European heritage, settled in central Ohio. Today, there remains a strong Southern influence in parts of Ohio.

Cincinnati was the first major city in the state. It was incorporated as a city in 1819. It attracted newcomers from the United States and western Europe. Many people came from Italy, lured by work in the city's surrounding mines and mills. In the 1830s, **immigrants** from Germany began to come to Cincinnati seeking economic opportunities. A strong German influence is still evident in parts of Cincinnati.

The tractor was introduced to Ohio in the early 1900s, making the difficult work of the early pioneers much easier.

Columbus grew steadily during the latter part of the twentieth century.

POPULATION

Close to 11.3 million people call Ohio home. About 88 percent of the population is of eastern, western, and central European heritage. African Americans make up 10 percent of the population, and the remaining 2 percent are Asian, Hispanic American, or Native American.

The most ethnically **diverse** region of Ohio is the northeast. This region encouraged the arrival of immigrants from Russia, eastern Europe, and Italy. Many early immigrants came to Ohio to work as laborers. Irish, German, and eastern-European immigrants made their way from the east to the nation's growing Midwest. Some of Ohio's African Americans are the ancestors of those who made it safely out of the south via the **Underground Railroad**.

Columbus is the state's largest city, with a population of about 636,000 people. Cleveland is the next largest, with a population of slightly more than 492,000. There are about 358,000 people in Cincinnati.

The Ohio State House was completed in 1861.

William McKinley

POLITICS AND GOVERNMENT

Ohio's government is divided into three branches. The legislative branch makes laws, the executive branch applies laws, and the judicial branch enforces and interprets laws. The governor of Ohio is the chief executive officer of state government. He or she is elected by the people for a four-year term. Among the governor's many responsibilities are proposing the state budget, and signing bills into laws.

Ohio is nicknamed "The Mother of Presidents" because a large number of United States presidents came from the state. Presidents Ulysses S. Grant, William McKinley, Rutherford B. Hayes, James A. Garfield, Benjamin Harrison, William H. Taft, and Warren G. Harding were all born in Ohio.

One of Ohio's most famous political figures was William McKinley, the twenty-fifth president of the United States. McKinley was elected in 1896, and was regarded as a strong and sympathetic leader. Unfortunately, he was **assassinated** five years after he became president.

The home of James A. Garfield, the twentieth president of the United States, became a national historic site on December 28, 1980.

The African American Heritage Festival is a week-long event, celebrated every May at the Ohio State University.

CULTURAL GROUPS

Ohio played an important role in the Underground Railroad and the **abolitionist** movement. Anti-slavery seeds sown in Ohio during the early 1800s helped ignite the American Civil War, resulting in the end of slavery. In Ripley, Ohio, there were many people who wanted to abolish slavery. John Rankin, pastor of the First Presbyterian Church in Ripley, helped hundreds of slaves escape. The first anti-slavery society was formed in 1835, and it helped as many as 2,000 runaway slaves during the years 1825 to 1865.

Many African Americans stayed in Ohio, while others went further north. Today, many African Americans celebrate their culture in Ohio. There is an African-American museum in Cleveland, and there are various festivals held throughout the state. Ohio State University hosts a large African-American heritage festival every year in May. This festival is a week-long celebration that features African and Caribbean food, music, and poetry.

QUICK FACTS

African-American men have had the right to vote in Ohio since 1870.

Toni Morrison, a well-known Ohioan, writes stories about the lives of African Americans.

In Cleveland, as many as forty languages were spoken during the nineteenth century.

Dolls are an important part of African culture, and may be found at some African-American celebrations, such as festivals.

Today, there are more Mennonites in Ohio than there are in their native land of Switzerland.

In 1810, the first person of the Amish faith settled in north-central Ohio. More followed from Switzerland. Today, about one-third of all Amish live in Ohio. There are at least twelve separate groups of Amish in the area, ranging from Old World Amish to Mennonites.

The Amish believe in distancing themselves from the outside world. Members are not allowed to participate in wars or hold public offices. They follow a simple, farm-based lifestyle. The Amish prefer to remain **self-sufficient**, avoiding technology such as electricity or telephones. The Mennonite faith, on the other hand, is less strict about the use of technology. Mennonites are allowed to use modern items such as automobiles.

The Amish are known for their large-scale barn raisings. A barn raising is a community event, and entire families pitch in to help. Traditionally, men build the barn while women prepare the feast. An entire barn can be built in one day without the use of modern equipment. The framing of the structure is usually completed before the lunchtime feast, and the rest is finished in the afternoon.

QUICK FACTS

The Amish are known for millwork, construction, woodworking, and farming with horse-drawn implements.

Irish dancing is a long-held tradition. At the Dublin Irish Festival in Dublin, Ohio, step dancers dazzle audiences with their fancy footwork.

Dublin, Ohio, attracts Irish people from all over the world to celebrate its annual Dublin Irish Festival. This festival features Irish games, dancing, and musical entertainment.

The Amish do not use advanced farm equipment, but rather rely on hand tools and horse-drawn plows.

The Marion Popcorn Festival is the largest festival of its kind in the world.

ARTS AND ENTERTAINMENT

Agricultural fairs take place in all corners of the state. Large crowds of Ohioans and tourists come to these county fairs to participate in activities like those of their ancestors—displaying homemade crafts, foods, prize hens, and cows. Festivals that showcase the state's agricultural goods include the Apple Butter Festival at Burton, the Marion Popcorn Festival, and the Reynoldsburg Tomato Festival.

On a larger scale, the Ohio State Fair, which has been in operation for over 150 years, draws about 1 million people through its gates each year. For two weeks in August, people come to see special exhibits and carnivals, and to experience the thrill of twirling around on amusement-park rides.

People can double their fun when they visit Twinsburg in August. A unique festival, called Twins Days, attracts twins from all over the United States to celebrate their unique family bonds.

QUICK FACTS

"The house that Jack built" was a house built at Bellaire, Ohio, in 1870. Jack was the mule who helped his master, Jacob Heatherington.

The legend of Annie Oakley is based on an Ohio woman named Phoebe Ann Moses. She was very handy with a gun and beat her talented husband in a target-shooting match. Oakley and her husband were featured in Buffalo Bill's Wild West Show.

Archibald Willard of Wellington painted *The Spirit of '76* in 1876. This image became a national icon.

At the annual Twins Days festival, each set of twins dress alike.

In 1993, Toni Morrison was awarded the Nobel Prize for Literature.

Many highly acclaimed writers hail from Ohio. One noted writer who lived in Cincinnati was Harriet Beecher Stowe, author of *Uncle Tom's Cabin*. President Abraham Lincoln called her "the little woman who started the big war." Her novel addressed slavery in the United States, raising awareness and concern over the **injustices** of this practice. Other famous Ohioan writers include Pulitzer-prize winner Toni Morrison, humorist James Thurber, and western author Zane Grey.

Cleveland is considered to be the home of rock and roll music, so it is in this city that the Rock and Roll Hall of Fame and Museum was built. Visitors can see John Lennon's Sergeant Pepper uniform and guitar, an outfit worn by Elvis Presley, and singer Janis Joplin's Porsche convertible.

QUICK FACTS

Science lovers can visit Thomas Edison's birthplace in Milan. This is the place where the famous inventor spent his early childhood.

The Cleveland Orchestra performs in Cleveland's beautiful Severance Hall. It is one of the world's greatest symphony orchestras.

Visitors to the Rock and Roll Hall of Fame and Museum will witness remarkable exhibits, films, videos, and artifacts.

SPORTS

Spelunking, or caving, is a popular activity in Ohio, with many clubs for people of all ages and skill levels.

Ohioans, as well as visitors to the state, have a variety of outdoor activities from which to choose. With the state's wealth of natural areas and state parks, many people enjoy camping, fishing, canoeing, and hiking. A popular destination for outdoor enthusiasts is Wayne National Forest, which stretches across 178,000 acres in the hills of southeastern Ohio. The area is comprised of the rugged foothills of the Appalachian Mountains, and is home to many lakes, rivers, and streams. Adventurers will likely spot wildlife, including deer, wild turkeys, and a variety of songbirds in the region.

A challenging sport, called spelunking, can be done in Ohio's Zane Caverns. Spelunkers descend into caves on ropes. Equipped with flashlights, they explore the dark crevices and crawlspaces of the caves. The Zane Caverns feature what seems like a bottomless pit as well as rock formations that resemble an owl, an alligator, and a human hand.

QUICK FACTS

Jesse Owens of Cleveland won four gold medals in the 1936 Olympics at Berlin.

Golf master Jack Nicklaus is from Ohio.

The National Football League began in Canton, Ohio in 1920. The Pro Football Hall of Fame is located there as well. At the Hall of Fame, visitors can see displays which include live action footage and a professional sports photography art gallery.

Ohio's many lakes and rivers provide opportunities for Ohioans to enjoy water sports such as canoeing.

QUICK FACTS

The Cleveland Cavaliers is Ohio's NBA franchise. The Cavaliers played their first game in Cleveland in 1970.

The Reds' home field is Cinergy Field in Cincinnati. They have played for Cincinnati since 1876 under various names. The team has been known as the Redlegs, the Red Stockings, and now, the Reds.

The Reds have won the World Series five times.

Ohio is a wonderful state for professional ball players and fans. There is a National Football League team, two Major League Baseball teams, and a National Basketball Association team.

The Cincinnati Bengals and the Cleveland Browns are NFL teams, and there is a heated rivalry between them. The Bengals play out of the new Paul Brown Stadium, and the Browns play in a new stadium on Lake Erie.

Ohio's Major League Baseball teams are the Cincinnati Reds and the Cleveland Indians. The Cleveland Indians have been Cleveland's team since 1915. They play out of Jacobs Field. The Cleveland Indians have won the World Series title twice—in 1920 and in 1948. They were the American League champions in 1997.

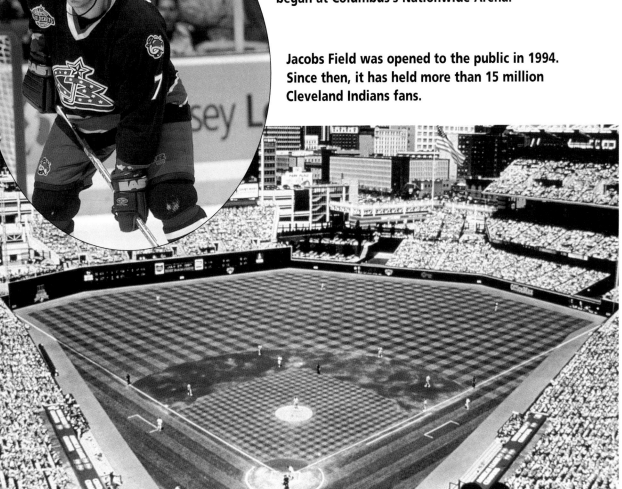

In 1997, Ohio was awarded a National Hockey League team. The Blue Jackets' first season, in 2000–2001, began at Columbus's Nationwide Arena.

Jacobs Field was opened to the public in 1994. Since then, it has held more than 15 million Cleveland Indians fans.

Brain Teasers

1

What was Ohio resident, Thomas Edison, famous for inventing?

a) the gasoline-powered car

b) the incandescent light bulb

c) the television

d) the computer

Answer: b) The incandescent light bulb

2

A well-known entertainer comes from Cleveland. Who is he?

Answer: Arsenio Hall. This late-night talk show host made his debut in the 1988 film, *Coming to America.*

3

Did Orville and Wilbur Wright fly the first aircraft in their home state of Ohio?

Answer: No. The brothers thought that Dayton's winds were too mild for their experiments, so they asked the U.S. Weather Bureau to help them find a better site. The brothers picked Kitty Hawk, an isolated village in North Carolina. Kitty Hawk provided high winds, tall dunes for gliding, and soft sand for landings.

4

Ohioans John Glenn and Neil Armstrong were what kind of explorers?

a) French explorers

b) fur traders

c) space explorers

d) explorers of the lost ark

Answer: c) Space explorers

5

There is a
Great Lake that
touches Ohio.
What is it called?

Answer: Lake Erie

6

What
baseball
game snack
was created
in Ohio?

Answer:
The hot dog.
Ohioan Harry M.
Stevens invented the hot
dog in 1900.

7

Who "jumped" into
the spotlight at the
1924 Olympic Games
in Paris?

Answer:
Ohioan and
long jumper
DeHart Hubbard
thrilled his home
state when he
became the first
African American to
win an Olympic gold
medal.

8

Cleveland is
said to be
the home of:

a) rock climbing

b) rock and roll

c) Rock Hudson

d) rock lobster

Answer: b) Rock and roll

FOR MORE INFORMATION

Books

Trager, James. *The People's Chronology: A Year-by-Year Record of Human Events from Prehistory to the Present.* New York: Holt, 1979.

Wills, Charles. *A Historical Album of Ohio.* Brookfield: Millbrook Press, 1996.

Wright, David K. *Ohio Handbook* (Moon Travel Handbooks). Emeryville: Moon, 1999.

Zimmerman, George and Carol. *Ohio.* Oldsaybrook: Globe Pequot, 1998.

Web sites

You can also go online and have a look at the following Web sites:

Ohio Division of Travel and Tourism
http://www.ohiotourism.com

The Edison Birthplace Museum
http://www.tomedison.org/

The Ohio Historical Society
http://www.ohiohistory.org/

The African-American Experience in Ohio
http://dbs.ohiohistory.org/africanam/

Ohio History Central Online Encyclopedia
http://www.ohiokids.org/ohc/index.html

Some Web sites stay current longer than others. To find other Ohio Web sites, enter search terms such as "Ohio," "Amish," "Cleveland," or any other topic you want to research.

GLOSSARY

abolitionist: a person who supported the termination of slavery in the United States

assassinated: murdered, often for political reasons

aviation: the design, development, production, and operation of aircraft

component: a part of a mechanical or electrical system

conifers: trees, such as evergreens and shrubs, that bear their seeds and pollen on separate, cone-shaped structures

diverse: different or varied

eligible: meeting the requirements to qualify

floriculture: the cultivation of flowers or flowering plants

front: where two dissimilar air masses meet

immigrants: people who move to another country

industrialization: the process of switching from a simple, agricultural way of life to mechanized industry

injustices: unfair actions

sect: a group of people who follow a particular religion

sedimentary: composed of organic matter and minerals

self-sufficient: able to supply one's own needs without external assistance

Underground Railroad: the southern Ohio route by which many slaves escaped from the bonds of slavery in the south to freedom in the north

unionized: workers organized to deal collectively with employers

Utopia: an ideal place with a perfect social system

vulcanize: the process that makes rubber hard and durable enough to use for vehicle tires

INDEX